Punctuation

John Butterworth

Illustrations by Lee Nicholls

OXFORD
UNIVERSITY PRESS

OXFORD

UNIVERSITY PRESS

Great Clarendon Street, Oxford OX2 6DP

Oxford University Press is a department of the University of Oxford.
It furthers the University's objective of excellence in research, scholarship,
and education by publishing worldwide in

Oxford New York

Auckland Bangkok Buenos Aires
Cape Town Chennai Dar es Salaam Delhi Hong Kong Istanbul
Karachi Kolkata Kuala Lumpur Madrid Melbourne Mexico City Mumbai
Nairobi São Paulo Shanghai Taipei Tokyo Toronto

Oxford is a registered trade mark of Oxford University Press
in the UK and in certain other countries

British Library Cataloguing in Publication Data available

ISBN 0–19–911161–8

1 3 5 7 9 10 8 6 4 2

Designed and Typeset by Mike Brain Graphic Design Limited
Printed in Hong Kong

Contents

Punctuation

When you write you put your thoughts into sentences. To show where your sentences begin and end, and how they should be read, you need **punctuation**.

Without any punctuation, writing would look like this:

1 chapter one jade come back sam yelled his voice was lost in the noise of the river tumbling under the bridge if you could call those two narrow planks and wobbly rail a bridge there was a large sign warning people that it wasn't safe danger it said but sams clown of a sister was already half-way across what should sam do he had two choices to go after her or run back to the camp-site and tell their mum and dad they had told jade and sam not to play near the river then he heard the loud splash that made his mind up for him

Try reading it. You will probably find this very difficult.

Here is the same bit of story.
Compare it with the first one. How many differences can you see?

2

CHAPTER ONE

"Jade, come *back*!" Sam yelled.

His voice was lost in the noise of the river, tumbling under the bridge – if you could call those two narrow planks and wobbly rail a "bridge". There was a large sign warning people that it wasn't safe. DANGER, it said; but Sam's clown of a sister, was already half-way across.

What should Sam do? He had two choices: to go after her, or run back to the camp-site and tell their mum and dad. (They had told Jade and Sam not to play near the river.) Then he heard the loud splash that made his mind up for him.

All the differences that you can find between pieces **1** and **2** are known as **punctuation**.

Speaking

Speaking is quite different from writing. In speaking you can add **expression** to what you say.

Expression means what you do with your voice, or with your hands and face, while you are talking. You can make your voice go up or down; you can make it loud or soft, You can pause. You can hesitate. You can repeat things.

When you talk, though, you don't have much time to think about it. The sentences can be quite muddled.

there was this girl . . . on the bridge . . . right . . . and a boy . . . shouting . . . er . . . come back . . . I think he shouted come back . . . it was difficult to hear with the river . . . you know . . . the river's going so fast and there's . . . noise and . . . all waves and that . . . and . . . then she's gone . . . just a splash . . .

This person tells the same story as the one on page 4, but it's quite different from a written story.

Try reading it aloud, with pauses where the dots are.

Writing

When you are writing you have lots of time. You can put everything tidily into sentences. You can go back and change things that you don't like.

But in writing there are no voices or faces or hands to give **expression**. Written words are just flat on the page. To bring it to life, you need these:

. ? ! : ; , – ( ) " "

They are called **punctuation marks**

Look back at the story on page 4, and see how many punctuation marks you can find.

Stop .

It's the smallest possible sign you can write – just a dot –
but it has one of the biggest jobs to do.

The Americans call it a **period**.
In French it's a **point**.

In German it's a **punkt**.
In English it's called a **full stop**.

Whether a sentence is short or long, it needs a full stop at the end.

 Jade slipped. She landed in the river with a splash.
She tried to swim to the bank, but the water was
flowing fast and swept her quickly downstream,
away from the bridge and straight towards the
rumbling thunder of Rushbrook Falls. She
tumbled down several small rapids, and over water-slides made of
smooth, slippery rock. It was a fast ride. If it hadn't been cold and
terrifying, it might have been fun.

How many sentences are there in this bit of story.
How short is the shortest? How long is the longest?

As well as ordinary full stops, there are two special full stops.
They come at the end of certain sentences.

? This is a **question mark**.
It's used only after questions.
Where's Jade? Is she all right?

! This is an **exclamation mark**.
It is used for sentences which have anger or surprise or urgency in them.
What a stupid thing to do! Look out!

➡You can find out more about questions and exclamations on pages 8 and 9.

Start with a capital letter

When you start a new sentence, you should use a capital letter.

The different letters are also known as **upper case** and **lower case**. In the old days printers kept the type in wooden cases, one above the other. The capital letters were in the upper case; the ordinary letters in the lower case.

Upper case:

A B C D E F G H I J K L M N O P Q R S T U V W X Y Z

Lower case:

a b c d e f g h i j k l m n o p q r s t u v w x y z

To get a capital letter on a keyboard, you have to hold down the **shift key** while you type. There is usually a shift key on each side of the letter keys. The sign on it is SHIFT or ⇧

Proper Nouns – Names

Proper nouns – the words which name people, places or things – also begin with a capital letter, wherever they come in a sentence.

Where is Jade?
There is a small footbridge over the River Rushbrook.
It was the last day of September.
Names in English begin with a capital letter.

Which words in these sentences are names? What are they names *of*?

I

The word *I* is always written as a capital, whether it's at the beginning of a sentence or not.

I warned her to be careful.
She said **I** was just being fussy.

Sentences

There are four main kinds of sentence:

1 Statements

These are sentences which tell you something:

There is a waterfall near the bridge.
It's dangerous to swim here.
Luckily Jade's brother heard her fall into the river.

Most statements end in a full stop, but sometimes, if they are meant with a lot of feeling, you can use an exclamation mark:

Jade's fallen in!

2 Questions

These are sentences which ask you something:

Where is the nearest telephone?
What happened?
Is there another bridge before the falls?

Questions, as you would expect, end with a question mark, and like all sentences they begin with a capital letter.

3 Commands

Commands tell you what to do – or not to do:

Stay away from the edge. Don't swim in the river.

An urgent or angry command can have an exclamation mark:

Hang on!
Don't ever do that again!

Commands can be very short – sometimes as short as one word:

Stop.   Go.   Run.   Swim.

Think of some more one-word commands.

4 Exclamations

These are sentences which say something with surprise or amusement or annoyance. Exclamations sound a bit like questions, but they don't need answering. They often begin with the words How... or What...

How stupid of her!   What a fool that girl is!
Was she *lucky* Sam heard her fall in!

And they always end in an exclamation mark. What a surprise!

Some statements and commands can also end with an exclamation mark. But don't overdo it, like the writer of this postcard.

Hi Liz,
Having a useless holiday! Weather's really yuk!! Fell in the river yesterday and got in big trouble!!! Don't forget to feed the goldfish! See you next week. Can't wait!!
Bye! Jade.

Long or Short

Sentences can be as short or as long as you like. These are short:

Jade fell off the bridge. She landed in the river.
The water was icy. The current was fierce.

Notice that even though they are short, they still need full stops between them.

This one is much longer and says much more.

Suddenly Jade slipped and fell off the bridge, down into the icy water of the river, where the fierce current swept her off her feet and carried her away downstream towards the wild rapids and the waterfall.

You can put as much information into one long sentence as you can put into several short ones.

Good writing is a mixture of short, medium, and long sentences.

Phrases and Clauses

There are lots of ways of making sentences longer. You can add extra **words** or extra **phrases**. Or you can join whole **sentences** together to make longer ones.

A sentence that is part of a longer sentence is called a **clause**.

Adding Phrases

A phrase is a group of words that makes sense but is not a sentence.

with a big splash   is a phrase

You could add it to the sentence: Jade fell into the river
to make a *new* sentence: Jade fell into the river with a big splash.

When you add a phrase to a sentence, it doesn't have to be on the end.

It could go at the beginning:
With a big splash Jade fell into the river.

Or even in the middle:
Jade fell, with a big splash, into the river.

You can add two or more phrases to the same main sentence:
All of a sudden, Jade fell, with a big splash, off the bridge into the river.

Because phrases are not sentences, they don't have their own capital letter and full stop. Don't write:
Jade fell off the bridge. With a big splash. **X**

This should not be two sentences; it should be one, with only one full stop.

You write it as it should be.

Joining Clauses

Whole sentences – clauses – can be added together to make longer ones, using words called **conjunctions**. Conjunctions are joining words.

The most common conjunction is **and**

The water was icy. The current was fierce.   2 sentences
⇨ The water was icy and the current was fierce.   1 sentence

There is no full stop before **and**, because a *conjunction* makes the two sentences into one.

There are lots of conjunctions – not just **and**. Some of the others are:

**or but because for when so as than before after
if like since until unless although whether while**

Jade fell off the bridge **because** it was slippery.

She tried to swim to the bank **but** the current was too strong.

She'd better get out **or** she'll be over the falls!

When Sam heard the splash, he ran to get help.

Unless he gets help quickly, it will be too late.

In the last two of these sentences the conjunction is at the beginning.
Find out whether all conjunctions can go at the
beginning – or only some of them.

Remember that a conjunction makes **one** sentence, not two. So don't write:

Jade fell off the bridge. Because it was slippery. ✗

When Sam heard the splash. He ran to get help. ✗

Comma ,

The job of the comma is to make sentences – particularly longer sentences – easier to read.

When you are reading aloud, commas usually mark a slight pause, or change of voice. Try reading the sentences on these two pages aloud, and *listening to the commas* in your voice.

Commas in Lists

When things are written in a list, they are called *items*. Instead of writing **and** between every item, you can use commas:

The shop on the campsite sold eggs, bacon, cheese, milk, lettuce, tomatoes, sausages, beans, cold drinks, and crisps.

Here is a list of the people and pets in Jade's family:

Jade, her brother, her mum, her dad, the dog, and a guinea-pig were all staying in a caravan in the Rushbrook Valley.

Here are lists of what Jade did, and how she felt, after falling in the river:

She bobbed, bounced, slithered, and tumbled down the rapids.
She felt cold, wet, foolish, and scared.

⬌ Some people leave out the last comma if it is followed by **and**. For example:

She felt cold, wet, foolish and scared.

It's up to you whether you put the last comma in or not. Look out for lists when you are reading, and see what different writers do.

Names and Descriptions

Often when you name someone, or something, you need a description as well. A comma is useful between the name and the description:

the Johnsons' dog, Wagger
Hulk, the guinea pig
Jade's brother, Sam

Which are the names here, and which are the descriptions?

Joins

Commas are also useful to show the *joins* in a sentence: for example, where a phrase or clause has been added, or two sentences made into one.

With a splash, Jade hit the water.
When she first fell in, she didn't know where she was.
The river was dangerous to swim in, although it wasn't deep.

Commas are particularly important when the sentence has an extra part stuck in the *middle*. When this happens there should be a comma *before* and *after* the extra part – like this:

Sam, who had heard the splash, ran to get help.
The waterfall, which he could hear in the distance, was the big danger.

What is the main sentence in each of these, and what is the extra part?

Commas and Conjunctions

⇔ Some writers put commas before conjunctions when sentences are joined, and some don't. The writer of these sentences *didn't*:

It wasn't deep but it was moving fast.
Did Jade jump in or did she fall?
Sam will have to get help before it's too late.

Rewrite these with a comma before the conjunction. Decide which you like better – comma, or no comma.

Semicolon ;

A semicolon marks a bigger break than a comma, but is not as final as a full stop.

Unlike a comma, a semicolon can go between two sentences. Use a semicolon if the sentences are alike, or belong together.

All rivers are dangerous; some are more dangerous than others.

The bridge is slippery; hold on tight.

She was cold; she was scared; she was wet.

Unlike full stops, semicolons can come in the middle of sentences. Use them only when you want a strong break between two parts of your sentence:

"She was told not to go near the river; but you know Jade!"

There was a loud splash; then a cry for help.

"I told her not to leave the campsite; I told her not to cross the river; and I told her to be back at the caravan by tea-time."

⇔ It's not always easy to know whether to use a comma, semicolon, or full stop. What matters is how you want your sentence, or sentences, to be read.

This short piece of writing has no punctuation except at the beginning and end.

The current was fast the water was cold Jade tried to swim it wasn't easy in her clothes.

Try reading it aloud a few times, and decide how *you* would punctuate it – and why.

Colon :

A colon is a special mark, with just a few special jobs.

You use a colon when you have a list of things coming after a *heading*.

A colon is used before giving an example – or examples – of something:

There's one thing Jade's good at: getting into trouble.

We did some exciting things: climbing, lots of swimming, kite-flying, and a trip on the mountain railway.

You also use a colon between two sentences, when the first one says something, and the second one says what you mean by it:

It isn't the first time Jade's been in trouble: last summer she climbed to the top of an enormous tree and couldn't get down.

Both times she was lucky: someone was there to help.

Colons are often found before instructions even if they are pictures:

How to light the barbecue:

There are lots of colons in this book, because it is full of examples and explanations. Find the colons on these two pages, and see for yourself what they do.

Where would you put a colon in this sentence?

Jade has only one person to blame herself.

Writing Speech

More than once Sam shouted at his sister to come back. The actual words he said were:

"Jade, come back."

To show that this is what someone is saying, we use speech marks before it and after it.

Speech marks look like commas, except that they are written above the line, and some are upside-down.

 When they are printed, speech marks look like the numbers **66** and **99**, and some people call them that. Another name for them is *inverted commas*. (*Inverted* means upside-down.) When you write the **66** it's called *opening* the speech marks. When you write the **99**, it's called *closing* the speech marks.

Inside the speech marks you put **speech only**, plus any punctuation that goes with it – full stop, exclamation mark, question mark or comma.

Phrases like, **he said … she said …** etc., all go *outside* the speech marks.

Look at the next bit of the story, and read aloud just the words people *said* – nothing else:

"Jade, come *back*!" Sam shouted.

There was a fisherman on the bank, sitting under a striped umbrella. "What's happening?" he asked.

Sam turned to him. "I need help. My sister's in the river. Do you know where there is a phone?"

"Yes," said the fisherman. "In my pocket."

You can do this with someone else, and make it sound like a conversation.

Using Speech Marks

Using speech marks is quite complicated. You need to follow these five steps:

Step 1 *Open* the speech marks: "

Step 2 Write the words that were spoken: "You're in luck

Step 3 Add ! ? , or .   "You're in luck,

Step 4 *Close* the speech marks: "You're in luck,"

Step 5 Carry on writing: "You're in luck," said the fisherman.

See how the five steps have been followed in this piece of conversation:

"You're in luck," explained the fisherman. "I've got a mobile phone."
"May I borrow it ?" asked Sam.
"Of course you can. Dial 999, and hurry !"

Which Punctuation?

There should always be a punctuation mark before the **99**. But which one?
Mostly it depends on what comes next:

"I've got a mobile phone."

This is a complete sentence, so you use a *full stop*.

"You're in luck," said the fisherman.

This is a sentence that carries on after the speech marks; so you use a comma.

BUT – after questions you write ... **?**" and after exclamations you write **!**"
whether the sentence carries on, or not.

"May I borrow it ?" asked Sam.
          ... Dial 999, and hurry !" said the fisherman.

The speech marks on these two pages are double ones: **"..."**
But speech marks don't have to be double. You will also see single ones: **'...'**
It doesn't matter which you use, as long as you don't keep changing between them.

Brackets ( )

Like speech marks, brackets come in pairs, with words, phrases, or sentences *inside* them.

(You use brackets like this.)

Inside brackets you put things that may be helpful, but not really necessary.

On page 4 there was a sentence in brackets:

> What should Sam do? He had two choices: to go after her, or run back to the campsite and tell their mum and dad. (They had told Jade and Sam not to play near the river.) Then he heard the loud splash that made his mind up for him.

Why do you think this sentence is in brackets?
What does the sentence in brackets *do*?
What would happen if it was left out?
Read the whole piece again without the bit in brackets, and see if it still makes sense.

Sometimes just *part* of a sentence is in brackets:

The Rushbrook (a shallow, fast moving river with several dangerous rapids) runs past the campsite.

It was lucky for Jade that there was someone (especially someone with a mobile phone) fishing on the river bank.

A small green island (with bushes and trees growing on it) stands a little way above the waterfall.

What do the bits in the brackets tell you?
Why are they in brackets?

Dash –

Dashes are sometimes used to mark a big break, or interruption, in a sentence:

Sam dialled 999 – not for the first time in his life.

Jade had to be rescued from a tree – less than a year ago.

A dash can be used like a colon:

"Which emergency service do you want – fire, police, or ambulance?"

Sometimes dashes are used instead of brackets:

The old footbridge – the one by the campsite – should have been repaired years ago.

Dashes are very useful in writing speech. Remember how speech is full of stops and starts and pauses (page 50). Dashes can show where these come.

Here are some of the things the fisherman said when he was telling the story to his own family:

"His sister had fallen in the river – so he said."

"Luckily I had the mobile phone with me – I nearly didn't take it today – so the lad was able to phone for help."

Dashes are also very useful for showing where someone is interrupted, and doesn't finish what they're saying:

"I've been telling them for years: that bridge is an accident waiting to – " Suddenly there was a knock on the door.

What do you think the fisherman was going to say next?

Apostrophe '

Sometimes on road signs, parts of long names are left out to save space.

Where do you think you would be going if you followed these signs?

B'ham   L'pool   S'hampton   N'castle   Manch'r   Sheff'd

The ' means some of the word has been left out.

Contraction

Many English words get pushed together to sound like one word. This is called **contraction**, and usually means some letters being left out.

For example,
do not ⇨ don't.   An o has been left out.
it is ⇨ it's   An i has been left out.
what has ⇨ what's   ha has been left out.

What's been left out in these *contractions*?

They're coming.   She's gone.   We've been really worried.
She'll be sorry.   I'd be careful.   Jade wasn't careful enough.

Possession – Belonging

's on the end of a word may mean something *belongs* to it.

Jade's shoes   the fisherman's phone   the river's steep banks

The shoes belong to Jade.
The phone belongs to the fisherman.
The banks belong to the river.

's and s'

Jade, **fisherman**, and **river** are all *singular* words. That means there is only one of each. *Plural words* – like **girls**, **fishermen**, or **rivers** – mean more than one.

For singular words you always show belonging by **'s**.
Some more examples are:

Jade's wet clothing
the dog's bowl
the bridge's dodgy railing

Sam's quick thinking
the guinea pig's hutch
the water's icy temperature

Even if a singular word already ends in **-s**, you still add **'s**:

Mr Banks's children
the bus's driver

the boss's car
the class's teacher

But

if the word ends in **-s** because it's *plural*, the apostrophe goes after it: **s'**

The shop is for the **campers**, so it's **the campers' shop.**
The car park is for **visitors**, so it's **the visitors' car park.**

If the word is plural but it *doesn't* end in **-s**, then stick to **'s**

The children's holidays.
Those people's caravan.

Don't make the common mistake of putting an apostrophe wherever you see an **s**. Most words that end in **-s** are just plain plurals like these words:

cats, dogs, bridges, fields, paths, holidays, caravans, tents …

The **-s** on the end is *not for belonging*, so there is **NO apostrophe!**

There is an odd-one-out you have to remember: **its**.

When **its** means there's something belonging to **it**, there's no apostrophe.
When **it's** short for **it is**, there is an apostrophe.

For example:
It's time you took the dog for **its** walk.

Paragraphs

Paragraphs are blocks of writing, sometimes as short as one sentence, but usually a few sentences long. The job of paragraphs is to break your writing up, making it easier to read and understand.

To mark the beginning of a new paragraph, you start a new line.

Read the piece of story on the opposite page. How many paragraphs are there?

New Face? New Place? ...

There are lots of reasons for starting a new paragraph, but usually it is because of some **change** in what you are writing about.

In the bit of writing opposite, there are three people. One is in the river, the other two are on the bank. When the story switches from the river to the bank, or from Jade to her brother, or from Sam to the fisherman, or back to the river, a new paragraph starts. This helps the reader to understand what's going on.

Paragraph 1

Paragraph 2

Paragraph 3

Paragraph 4

Paragraph 5

CHAPTER TWO

Meanwhile, what was Jade doing? She *tried* to do three things, very quickly, one after the other. First she tried to stand up, since the water was quite shallow; but before she knew it, the fierce current had knocked her off her feet. Next she tried to swim, but the power of the water made that impossible: she was swept out into the middle of the river, and away down the rapids like a bobbing cork. Lastly she tried to shout for help, but with the roar of the water – well, you can imagine.

What Jade didn't know was that Sam had seen it all happen. He ran, as fast as his young legs would carry him, down the bank and along the riverside path. He didn't know how he would help; he just knew that he had to do something, and do it fast. It was just a stroke of luck that he saw the fisherman, sitting under his striped umbrella.

The fisherman had had a bad morning. Not one fish had bitten his line, and he was thinking seriously of packing up for the day. He didn't see Jade shoot past because she was hidden by some rocks. But he did hear Sam shouting to her: "Jade, come back." He looked up to see a frightened boy running towards him.

As if Jade *could* come back! Jade couldn't even stop. It was bad enough where she was, but around the next bend of the river, it became even wilder, with dips and drops and tumbling white waves. The banks were steep and rocky. At one point the stream divided into two branches, with a tall rocky island in between. Jade saw it ahead and wondered which side the stream would take her. Not that it mattered much. Both sides ended up at the same place: the place where the river disappeared altogether, and plunged over Rushbrook Falls.

"Help!" called Jade again. But only a heron, standing at the edge on one leg, heard her as she whisked by. It opened its big, grey-blue wings and flapped heavily away.

More about paragraphs

Paragraphs can be used to show changes of **time** – as well as changes of **people** and **places**. If the writer jumps ahead in time, or back in time, there should be a new paragraph.

You often see paragraphs beginning with phrases like :

Next day …   Later that morning …

When she was much younger …   A long time ago …

Look at the next bit in the story. Where is the jump in time, and how long is it?

The island was now straight ahead of her. It was round, green, and grassy, worn smooth by the water, but on the right-hand side there were trees and bushes growing, some with low branches that stuck out over the water. Jade thought that if she could grab one of them she could pull herself out. She started to swim to the right. The island loomed. The river split. Jade made one last, huge effort. One branch shot past, too high. The next one snapped as she grabbed it. The third one held. And so did Jade.

Two minutes later she was sitting on a large rock, soaking wet and shivering with the cold – but safe. And there on the bank was Sam, waving at her and holding something that looked like a small radio. It was the fisherman's mobile phone.

⇔ There are no fixed rules to tell you how many paragraphs a piece of writing should have. It is very much up to you – the writer – to decide.

When you are reading, look at what other writers do. Ask yourself questions like, Why is this a new paragraph? What was that paragraph about? What change is the writer making here?

Indent

When you start a new paragraph, you start a new line. You can also begin the new paragraph a little way over to the right. The space between the margin and the first word of the paragraph is called an **indent.**

indent

 "Help!" called Jade again. But only a heron, standing at the edge on one leg, heard her as she whisked by. It opened its big, grey-blue wings and flapped heavily away.

Dialogue – Conversation

What people say to each other in a story is called **dialogue**. This is pronounced *dialog* and just means conversation.

When you write dialogue you need speech marks to show what is being said.

(➔You can find out all about speech marks on pages 16 and 17.)

But it is also helpful to use paragraphs to show who is speaking.

This conversation was shouted across the river:

Change of speaker, new paragraphs

"Jade," yelled Sam, "are you all right?"

"Yes," she answered. "I'm fine. How did you know I was here?"

"I saw you fall in, and followed you."

"Sam, you're so clever."

"*You're* not," Sam said. "You're going to be in big trouble when you get back."

Same speaker, same paragraph

Jade shrugged her shoulders. "It won't be the first time," she said. She looked around and saw water on all sides. "What bothers me right now is how I'm going to get off here. You may not have noticed, but this is an island."

Notice that there is a new paragraph every time the speaker changes, from Jade to Sam and back to Jade, etc. It means there are lots of very short paragraphs, but it helps the reader to follow the conversation.

Writing Play Scripts

When you act in a play or film, you are given a **script**. In the script are **directions** – which tell the actors and producer what to *do*; and **lines**, which tell the actors what to *say*.

Jade is standing on the rock. Her brother is on the bank. It is difficult to hear because of the noise of the water, so they are both shouting.

SAM   Jade, are you all right?

JADE   Yes, I'm fine. How did you know I was here?

SAM   I saw you fall in, and followed you.

JADE   Sam, you're so clever.

SAM   *You're* not. You're going to be in big trouble when you get back.

JADE   (*shrugging her shoulders*) It won't be the first time.

She looks around and sees water on all sides.

What bothers me right now is how I'm going to get off here. You may not have noticed, but this is an island.

SAM   (*holding up the mobile phone to show Jade*)

Don't worry. I've made a 999 call. Help's on its way. Be here any minute.

While Sam is speaking, there is the sound of a helicopter approaching. Both the children look up. The camera zooms in on the helicopter as it hovers overhead. A policewoman in a blue helmet comes down on a rope.

Writing Addresses

When you send a letter to someone, you write their address on the envelope. Addresses have special punctuation: each part of the address begins on a new line.

There are two ways to write addresses. You can choose:

Jade Johnson,
   14, Heron Road,
      OXFORD,
         OX21 3XO

Jade Johnson
14 Heron Road
OXFORD
OX21 3XO

This is how everyone used to write addresses before the days of computers. Many people still do, and it looks smart.

When computers print addresses they look like this. Now lots of people *write* addresses this way, too.

How many differences can you see between the old way and the new way? Which one do you like better?

....

Letters

When you write a letter to someone you should put your address and the date – but not your name – at the top, on the right-hand side. This is so the receiver will know where to write back to.

Here is the letter Jade wrote to the policewoman who rescued her from the island:

your address, top right ----- *14, Heron Road,*

                     OXFORD,   **date, below the address**

                  OX21 3XO

comma here   *5th September, 1999*

Dear Sergeant Shotter,

Thank you very much for rescuing me from the river and for coming so quickly. It was fun being lifted into the helicopter, but it wasn't fun being in the water. I know I am a very lucky girl, and I will be more careful next time. **comma here**

Yours sincerely,
Jade Johnson

Big and Bold

Every page in this book has a heading. Headings have to stand out, catch attention, so they are often in big type or **bold** type – or **both**.

Headings work best if they are on a separate line, with the next line left clear:

On a computer or word processor, you can make your headings stand out by choosing a different *font-size* for the letters.

A lot of computers have menus like this:

click here to make letters bigger **click here to make them bold**

| Somefont | ▼ | | 12 | ▼ | | **B** | *I* | U |

When you are writing, you make a heading stand out by underlining it – <u>with a ruler</u>.

How to Write a Heading

Notice that in a heading, all the *main* words begin with a capital letter.

....

Emphasis

Sometimes in your writing you want some words to have more importance than others, or to stand out in some way. This is called **emphasis**. Here are some of the different ways words can be emphasized:

bold *italic* ***bold and italic*** <u>underlined</u>

It wasn't just cold in the river, it was absolutely *freezing*!
Every sentence should end with a ***full stop***.
"Never mind <u>when</u> I get off this island. Tell me <u>how</u> I get off."

Which words have been emphasized?
Why do you think they are emphasized?

How do you emphasize a word when you are *speaking*?

Headlines

Newspaper writers – called *journalists* – often use headlines like these to attract the readers' interest.

River rescue drama

Lucky Jade Johnson, 9, was lifted to safety yesterday by a police helicopter near the fearsome Rushbrook Falls. She scrambled out of the water just feet from the brink, only to find herself stranded on a small island in the middle of the rapids. It was her quick-thinking brother, Sam, who raised the alarm.

Heard a Splash

Eight-year-old Sam says he didn't see what happened, but he heard a splash, and knew his sister was in trouble …

Think of some other headlines you could use for a news story about Jade's adventure.

Making a Point

Some writing is not written in sentences one after the other. It is cut up into separate points that look like short paragraphs.

Riverside campsite – *giving you the best*

- Great for family holidays
- Tents and caravans welcome
- Clean, modern toilet and shower blocks
- Large children's play area
- River and spectacular waterfall nearby

The black dots are called '*bullets*'. Each line is a '*bullet point*'.

What advantage can you see in using bullet points for this kind of writing?

Punctuating Poetry

Poets like to be different. They sometimes use punctuation in very unusual ways. Some don't use it at all.

The usual way to write poetry is in lines and verses. The first word on each line begins with a capital letter, even if it isn't the start of a sentence. Poets often use different indents to give their verses a 'shape'.

Who has seen the wind?   `Lines`
Neither I nor you:
But when the leaves are trembling
The wind is passing through.

Who has seen the wind?
Neither you nor I
But when the trees bow down their heads   `verses`
The wind is passing by.

Christina Rossetti

Having Fun

Not all writing has to be serious. And not all writing has to keep to the rules. Especially poetry. In poetry you can use words – and punctuation – to create ideas and pictures in almost any way you like.

So, now that you've got to the end of the book and learnt all these rules, have some fun breaking them – like Jade did when her teacher asked the class to write about their holidays.

through, the (rapids; wild) — 'and: ov! er t h e dr o p the river, keeps tumbling? without a ●

Jade Johnson
Trust Jade!

Index